# GRAPHIC SURVIVAL STORIES

# DEFYING DEATH IN THE
# MOUNTAINS

*by* Rob Shone

*illustrated by* Nick Spender

rosen publishing's
**rosen
central**

New York

Published in 2010 by The Rosen Publishing Group, Inc.
29 East 21st Street, New York, NY 10010

Designed and produced by
David West Books

*Editor:* Katharine Pethick

Photo credits:
P5m, Jan van der Crabben; 6b, Walter Siegmund; 7m, Nolispamno; 44t, Muddymorn; 45t, papalars.

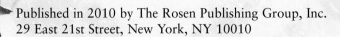

### Library of Congress Cataloging-in-Publication Data

Shone, Rob.
 Defying death in the mountains / Rob Shone ; illustrated by Nick Spender.
    p. cm. --  (Graphic survival stories)
 Includes index.
 ISBN 978-1-4358-3532-0 (library binding) -- ISBN 978-1-61532-866-6 (pbk.) -- ISBN 978-1-61532-868-0 (6-pack)
 1.  Mountaineering--Juvenile literature. 2.  Wilderness survival--Juvenile literature.  I. Spender, Nik, ill. II. Title.
 GV200.S53 2010
 796.52'2--dc22

                              2009041568

Manufactured in China

CPSIA Compliance Information: Batch #DW0102YA:
For Further Information contact Rosen Publishing, New York, New York at 1-800-237-9932

# CONTENTS

# MAJESTIC MOUNTAINS

*At 29,029 feet (8,848 m) high, Mount Everest is the world's tallest mountain above sea level.*

**A** quarter of the Earth's surface is mountainous but only a tenth of the world's population lives in mountain regions. Because of their isolation, many ranges are still in a natural unspoiled state.

*THE APPALACHIANS*

*THE ROCKY MOUNTAINS*

**THE WORLD'S MAJOR MOUNTAIN RANGES**

*THE ALPS*

*THE HIMALAYAS*

*The sport of rock climbing first became popular during the 1920s.*

*THE ANDES*

## MOUNTAIN TYPES

Seventy million years ago India collided with the Asian landmass crumpling and lifting the Earth's crust into what today are called the Himalayas. The mountains of the Himalayas are fold mountains. Other examples can be found in the South American Andes and the Alps in Europe. Fault-block mountains are formed when the bedrock is broken and forced upward. The East African rift valley is an example. Mountains can also be formed by volcanic action, such as Mount Fuji in Japan. A fourth type is called monadnock or inselberg mountains. These are small isolated mountains that rise from the surrounding plains. Sugarloaf Mountain in Brazil is an example.

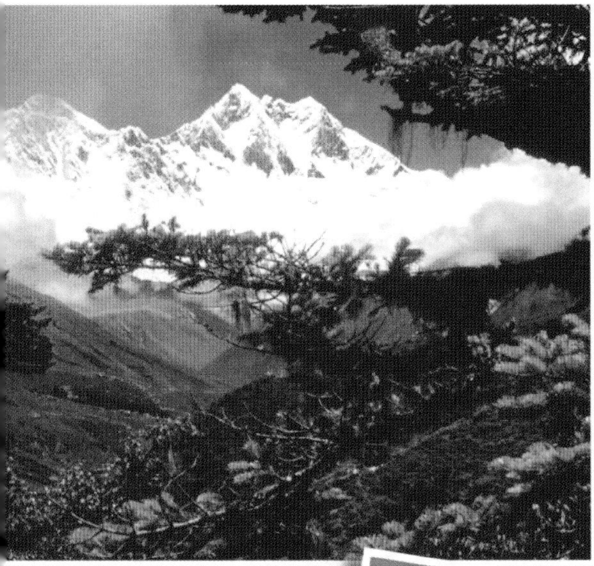

## Total Height

Although the summit of Mount Everest is the highest point on Earth by some definitions, it is not the tallest mountain. Mauna Kea in Hawaii stands 13,803 feet (4,207 m) above sea level but its base is 19,673 feet (5,996 m) below sea level, giving it a total height of 33,476 feet (10,203 m), 4,447 feet (1,355 m) taller than Everest.

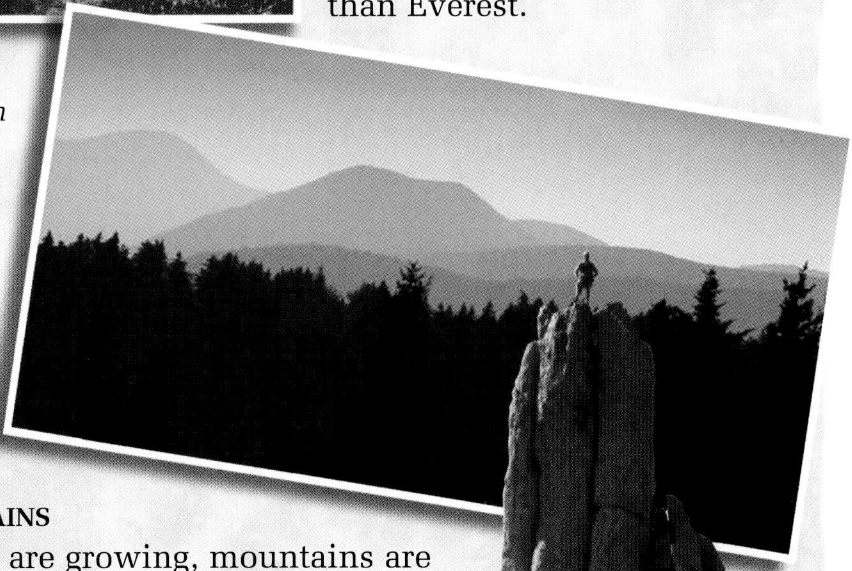

*The Blue Ridge Mountains in North America's Appalachian Mountain range are 480 million years old. In that time erosion has worn them down and rounded their summits.*

## Shaping Mountains

Even while they are growing, mountains are being worn down by a process called erosion. Water has the greatest effect. It can shatter rock by freezing and expanding in tiny cracks. Streams can carry gravel and sand that grind down their rocky slopes. Glaciers, slow-moving rivers of ice, gouge huge chunks from mountainsides. Avalanches, rockfalls, and vegetation all play a part in shaping mountains.

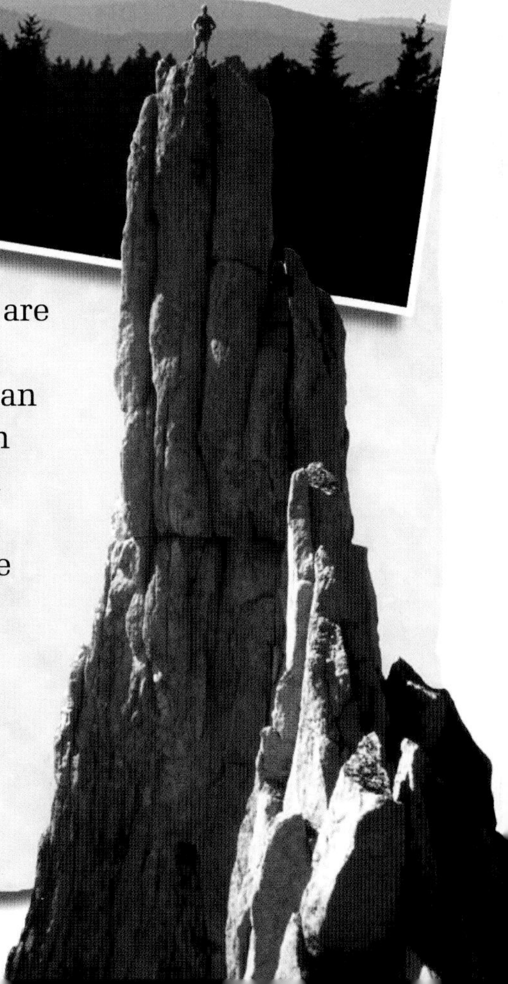

*Erosion can create some spectacular and fantastic rock shapes, as in this peak in Yosemite National Park, California.*

# MOUNTAIN SURVIVAL

*Crampons and ice axes are vital when scaling walls of ice.*

**In 1953 Edmund Hillary and Tenzing Norgay became the first people to stand on the summit of Mount Everest. Today dozens of climbers a year reach the mountain's top.**

### GROWTH IN POPULARITY

In 1854 Sir Alfred Wills climbed the Wetterhorn in the Swiss Alps, marking the birth of modern mountaineering. Since then mountain regions have become more and more popular with athletes and tourists. Activities such as rock climbing, skiing, snowboarding, and trekking have become commonplace. People can now get to mountainous areas that were once difficult to reach. As a result, mountain rescue teams are kept busy.

*The High Sierra in eastern California is popular with skiers and trekkers. Much of the mountain range is protected by law.*

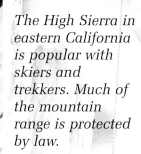

*Some animals are born mountaineers. The Rocky Mountain goat has specially adapted feet to help it clamber up and down steep mountain slopes.*

## DANGERS

Mountains can be perilous places from top to bottom. Above 23,000 feet (7,010 m) there is not enough air for anyone to survive for long. A shortage of oxygen can cause the brain to swell and the lungs to fill with fluid, followed by death. Hazards also exist lower down. Rockfalls, avalanches, and hidden crevasses can bury and swallow up the unwary climber. There is also the danger of falling, caused by carelessness or equipment failure.

## SURVIVAL TIPS

- **WEAR LAYERED CLOTHING.** The temperature high in the mountains can vary greatly. A hot day can turn into a freezing night.
- **COMMUNICATION** Tell people where you are going and when you are coming back.
- **STAY WHERE YOU ARE.** If you get lost, do not move. You will be easier to find.
- **CARRY A SURVIVAL PACK.** A good pack should contain a first-aid kit, waterproof matches, a whistle, and spare clothes.
- **AVALANCHES** If you get caught in an avalanche, use a swimming motion to stay at the top of the slide, and get rid of anything that could drag you down the slide, such as a backpack.

*There are several types of avalanches (left), and they are all deadly. Avalanche emergency and rescue equipment (above) includes, left to right, an airbag system, a collapsed probe, a shovel, and an avalanche beacon. The airbag is designed to inflate in an avalanche, keeping the victim on the surface of the snow.*

# FLIGHT FIVE-SEVEN-ONE
## The Andes, Argentina, South America, 1972

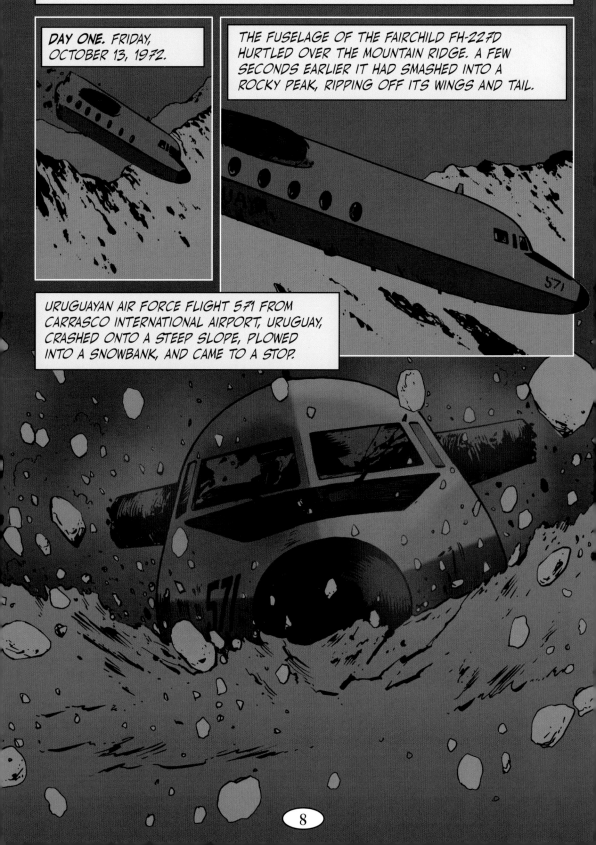

DAY ONE. FRIDAY, OCTOBER 13, 1972.

THE FUSELAGE OF THE FAIRCHILD FH-227D HURTLED OVER THE MOUNTAIN RIDGE. A FEW SECONDS EARLIER IT HAD SMASHED INTO A ROCKY PEAK, RIPPING OFF ITS WINGS AND TAIL.

URUGUAYAN AIR FORCE FLIGHT 571 FROM CARRASCO INTERNATIONAL AIRPORT, URUGUAY, CRASHED ONTO A STEEP SLOPE, PLOWED INTO A SNOWBANK, AND CAME TO A STOP.

THE AIRPLANE HAD BEEN CARRYING MEMBERS OF A RUGBY CLUB TO SANTIAGO, CHILE, WHERE THEY WERE GOING TO PLAY A GAME. HOWEVER, BAD WEATHER HAD DRIVEN THE PLANE OFF COURSE. WHEN IT CRASHED INTO THE ANDEAN MOUNTAINS, NO ONE KNEW EXACTLY WHERE THEY WERE.

**DAY TWO.** OF THE 40 PASSENGERS AND FIVE CREW MEMBERS, TWELVE PEOPLE DIED IN THE CRASH AND FIVE MORE WERE MISSING, LEAVING 28 SURVIVORS.

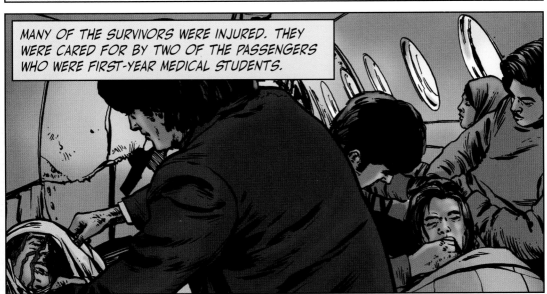

MANY OF THE SURVIVORS WERE INJURED. THEY WERE CARED FOR BY TWO OF THE PASSENGERS WHO WERE FIRST-YEAR MEDICAL STUDENTS.

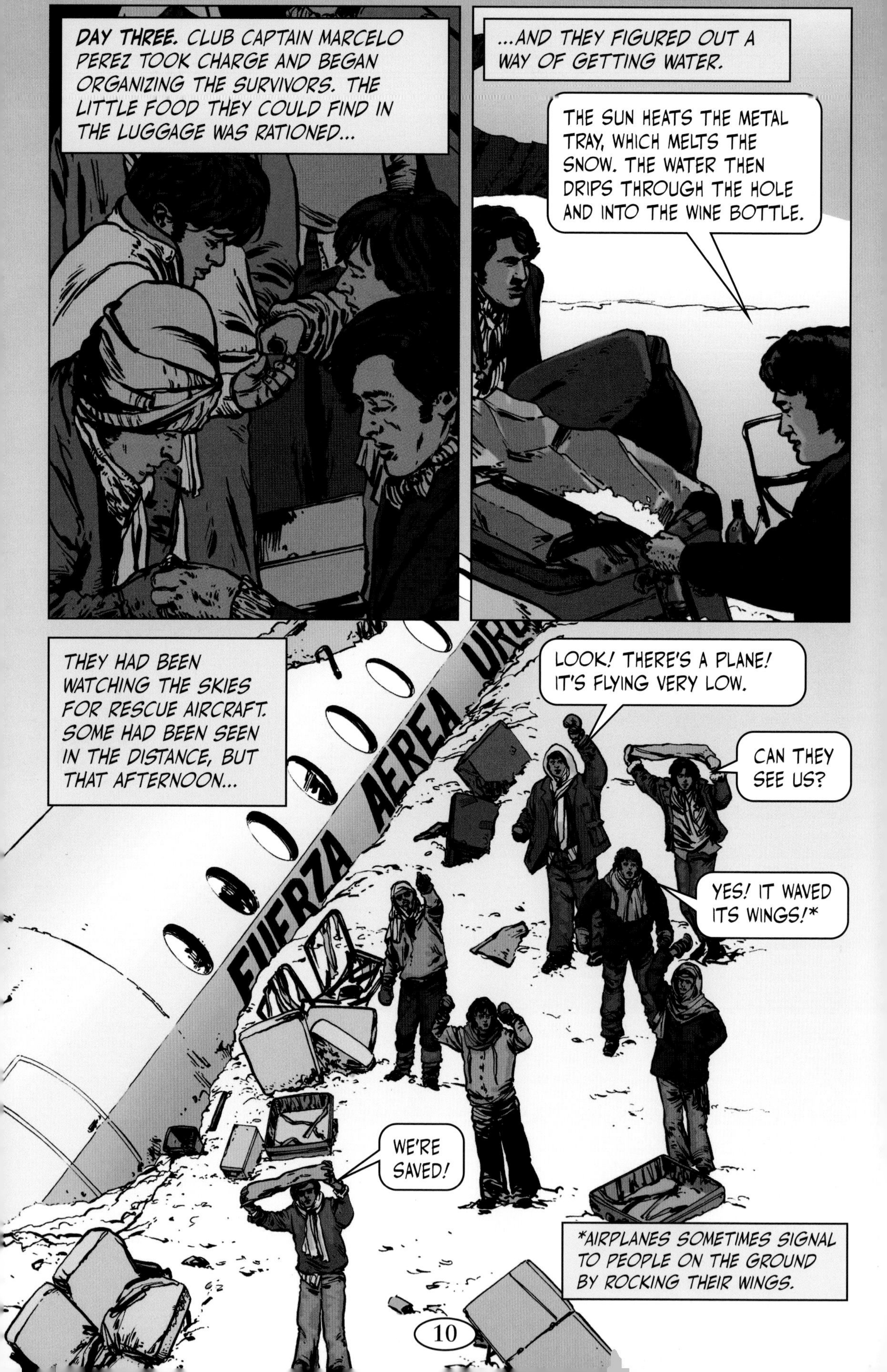
DAY THREE. CLUB CAPTAIN MARCELO PEREZ TOOK CHARGE AND BEGAN ORGANIZING THE SURVIVORS. THE LITTLE FOOD THEY COULD FIND IN THE LUGGAGE WAS RATIONED...
...AND THEY FIGURED OUT A WAY OF GETTING WATER.
THE SUN HEATS THE METAL TRAY, WHICH MELTS THE SNOW. THE WATER THEN DRIPS THROUGH THE HOLE AND INTO THE WINE BOTTLE.
THEY HAD BEEN WATCHING THE SKIES FOR RESCUE AIRCRAFT. SOME HAD BEEN SEEN IN THE DISTANCE, BUT THAT AFTERNOON...
LOOK! THERE'S A PLANE! IT'S FLYING VERY LOW.
CAN THEY SEE US?
YES! IT WAVED ITS WINGS!*
FUERZA AEREA
WE'RE SAVED!
*AIRPLANES SOMETIMES SIGNAL TO PEOPLE ON THE GROUND BY ROCKING THEIR WINGS.

LATER...

SOMEONE'S BEEN STEALING FOOD!

I HAD SOME. I WAS HUNGRY.

SO DID I.

AND ME.

WHAT DOES IT MATTER, MARCELO? WE'LL BE OUT OF HERE BY THIS TIME TOMORROW.

THE RESCUERS DID NOT COME, THOUGH, AND THEY HAD USED UP MUCH OF THEIR FOOD.

DAY TEN. SUSANA PARRADO HAD DIED THE DAY BEFORE, LEAVING 27 SURVIVORS. WITH ALL THEIR FOOD GONE, THEY CALLED A MEETING.

WE HAVE TO FACE FACTS. WE HAVE NO FOOD, AND THERE IS NONE TO BE HAD.

WE DON'T HAVE AN ALTERNATIVE. IF WE WANT TO LIVE...

...WE ARE GOING TO HAVE TO EAT OUR DEAD FRIENDS.

11

THE BODIES OF THE DEAD HAD BEEN PLACED NEXT TO THE PLANE.

ROBERTO CANESSA WAS THE FIRST TO EAT MEAT FROM ONE OF THE FROZEN CORPSES.

OTHERS FOLLOWED HIS EXAMPLE.

EVENTUALLY EVERYONE ATE FROM THE VICTIMS OF THE CRASH.

DAY ELEVEN. A TRANSISTOR RADIO HAD KEPT THE SURVIVORS IN TOUCH WITH THE OUTSIDE WORLD.

THAT'S IT, FERNANDO. WE'RE DONE FOR.

THE GOVERNMENT HAS JUST ANNOUNCED THAT THE SEARCH FOR FLIGHT 571, THAT WENT MISSING ELEVEN DAYS AGO IN THE ANDES, HAS BEEN CALLED OFF.

WELL, IF THEY'RE NOT COMING TO GET US, WE'LL JUST HAVE TO GET OUT ON OUR OWN.

THE SAME DAY, THREE OF THE SURVIVORS HAD CLIMBED INTO THE MOUNTAINS IN SEARCH OF THE AIRPLANE'S TAIL. THEY SPENT THE NIGHT IN THE OPEN AND NEARLY FROZE TO DEATH.

THE NEXT DAY THEY FOUND THE BODIES OF FIVE MISSING PEOPLE, BUT NOT THE TAIL SECTION.

DAY 17. THE SURVIVORS WERE HUDDLED IN THE FUSELAGE, PREPARING TO SPEND ANOTHER NIGHT ON THE MOUNTAIN, WHILE OUTSIDE A STORM RAGED.

A NOISE COMING FROM OUTSIDE WOKE SOME OF THE SLEEPERS.

IS THAT THUNDER?

AN AVALANCHE SWEPT DOWN THE MOUNTAINSIDE...

...AND SMASHED INTO THE AIRPLANE, FILLING IT WITH SNOW.

14

THE SURVIVORS CLAWED FRANTICALLY AT THE PACKED SNOW, TRYING TO FREE THOSE WHO HAD BEEN BURIED.

DAY 20. AFTER THREE DAYS THE STORM DIED DOWN. THE SURVIVORS DUG THEMSELVES OUT INTO THE FRESH AIR.

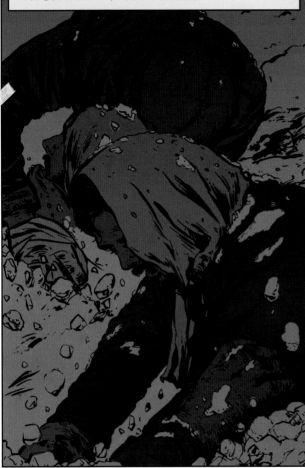

THE AIRPLANE HAD BEEN COMPLETELY COVERED BY SNOW. THE SURVIVORS GOT TO WORK DIGGING IT OUT. EIGHT PEOPLE HAD BEEN KILLED BY THE AVALANCHE, INCLUDING MARCELO PEREZ.

DAY 36. ON NOVEMBER 17, ROBERTO CANESSA, FERNANDO PARRADO, AND ANTONIO VIZINTIN SET OUT TO FIND A WAY OVER THE MOUNTAINS AND INTO CHILE. INSTEAD OF THE PATH TO CHILE, THEY FOUND THE TAIL SECTION. LUGGAGE WAS SCATTERED OVER THE SNOW, CONTAINING FOOD AND WARM CLOTHING. THEY ALSO FOUND THE AIRPLANE'S BATTERIES.

57

WITH THE BATTERIES THEY COULD POWER THE AIRPLANE'S RADIO AND CONTACT SANTIAGO. THEY SPENT THE NIGHT IN THE TAIL TO DECIDE WHAT THEY SHOULD DO NEXT.

THE BATTERIES ARE TOO HEAVY TO CARRY, SO WE SHOULD BRING THE RADIO BACK HERE.

ROY HARLEY SHOULD COME, TOO. HE KNOWS HOW RADIOS WORK.

DAY 43. CANESSA, PARRADO, VIZINTIN, AND HARLEY TREKKED BACK TO THE TAIL WITH THE RADIO. THEY SPENT THE NEXT FIVE DAYS TRYING TO GET IT TO WORK, WITHOUT SUCCESS.

IT LOOKS LIKE WE'RE GOING TO HAVE TO WALK OUT OF HERE AFTER ALL.

MEANWHILE, THE PROBLEM OF SLEEPING OUTSIDE AT NIGHT IN THE COLD MOUNTAINS WAS SOLVED BY CARLOS PAEZ RODRIGUEZ. HE SEWED INSULATING MATERIAL TOGETHER TO MAKE A PATCHWORK QUILT SLEEPING BAG LARGE ENOUGH FOR THREE PEOPLE.

DAY 61. ON TUESDAY, DECEMBER 12, CANESSA, PARRADO, AND VIZINTIN SET OUT ONCE MORE FOR CHILE. THIS TIME THEY HAD THE SLEEPING BAG. ONLY 16 OF THE ORIGINAL 45 PASSENGERS AND CREW WERE LEFT ALIVE.

THROUGHOUT THE DAY THEY CLIMBED STEADILY UP THE MOUNTAIN RANGE THAT OVERLOOKED THE WRECK. AT NIGHT THE SLEEPING BAG PROTECTED THEM FROM THE FREEZING COLD.

DAY 63. THE NEXT DAY THE CLIMBERS REACHED THE TOP OF THE MOUNTAIN. INSTEAD OF GREEN VALLEYS, THEY SAW MOUNTAIN RANGE AFTER MOUNTAIN RANGE. CANESSA THOUGHT HE SAW A ROAD IN THE DISTANCE.

THERE! I THINK IT'S A WAY THROUGH.

THEY DECIDED THAT VIZINTIN WOULD LEAVE HIS SHARE OF THE FOOD AND GO BACK TO THE PLANE, WHILE CANESSA AND PARRADO PRESSED ON.

DAY 66. BY DECEMBER 18, CANESSA AND PARRADO HAD CROSSED THE LAST MOUNTAIN RANGE AND STARTED THE DESCENT INTO CHILE.

DAY 69. ON DECEMBER 20, CANESSA AND PARRADO, EXHAUSTED AND UNABLE TO GO ON, ATTRACTED THE ATTENTION OF THREE CHILEAN COWBOYS. THE NEXT DAY THEY WERE RESCUED BY CHILEAN OFFICIALS.

DAY 72. AT 10:00 A.M. ON SATURDAY, DECEMBER 23, HELICOPTERS ARRIVED AT THE CRASH SITE. SIX SURVIVORS HAD BEEN TAKEN TO SAFETY THE DAY BEFORE. AT LAST, THE REMAINING EIGHT WERE ABLE TO LEAVE.

THE END

# BACK FROM THE DEAD
## JOE SIMPSON, SIULA GRANDE, THE PERUVIAN ANDES, SOUTH AMERICA, 1985

THE MOST DANGEROUS PART OF CLIMBING A MOUNTAIN IS GETTING BACK DOWN. THE MAJORITY OF ACCIDENTS HAPPEN DURING THE DESCENT. JOE SIMPSON AND SIMON YATES HAD SPENT THREE DAYS CLIMBING THE 20,813-FOOT (6,344-M) TALL SIULA GRANDE. THEY HAD RUN OUT OF FUEL AND NEEDED TO GET BACK TO THEIR CAMP AS QUICKLY AS POSSIBLE.

SIMPSON WAS LEADING. HE WAS TRYING TO CLIMB DOWN AN ICE WALL USING HIS ICE AXES AS ANCHORS WHEN...

...THE ICE GAVE WAY.

AHHH!

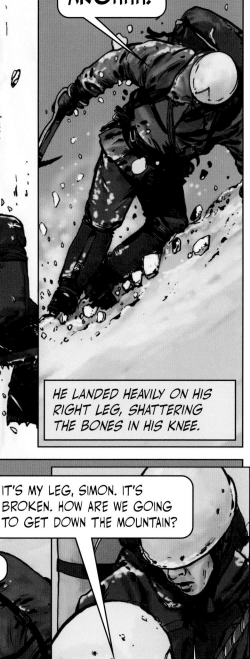

ARGHHH!

HE LANDED HEAVILY ON HIS RIGHT LEG, SHATTERING THE BONES IN HIS KNEE.

SIMON YATES CLIMBED DOWN THE ICE WALL. HE COULD TELL THAT SIMPSON HAD BEEN SERIOUSLY INJURED AND THAT THEY WERE IN TROUBLE.

JOE! ARE YOU OKAY?

IT'S MY LEG, SIMON. IT'S BROKEN. HOW ARE WE GOING TO GET DOWN THE MOUNTAIN?

DON'T WORRY. WE'LL FIND A WAY OF GETTING YOU BACK.

YATES COULD NOT LEAVE SIMPSON THERE. HE WOULD HAVE DIED BEFORE HELP ARRIVED. THEY WORKED OUT A PLAN. YATES, ANCHORED IN A SNOW SEAT, LOWERED SIMPSON DOWN THE MOUNTAIN AS FAR AS THEIR ROPE WOULD ALLOW AND THEN CLIMBED DOWN TO HIM. THEY REPEATED THE TASK AGAIN AND AGAIN.

IT WAS GETTING DARK, BUT THE HARDEST PART WAS NEARLY OVER. SUDDENLY, SIMPSON FELT THAT SOMETHING WAS WRONG.

THE SLOPE – IT'S GETTING STEEPER. I'M GOING TOO FAST!

SIMPSON WAS SLIDING FASTER AND FASTER DOWN THE SLOPE. THE DESCENT WAS GETTING OUT OF CONTROL.

SIMON! STOP!

YATES COULD NOT HEAR SIMPSON ABOVE THE WIND AND CONTINUED LOWERING HIM.

OOF! I HOPE JOE TAKES THE WEIGHT OFF THE ROPE SOON. THIS SNOW SEAT ISN'T GOING TO LAST FOREVER.

YATES LOWERED HIM OVER THE EDGE OF A CLIFF. SIMPSON TRIED TO CLIMB UP THE ROPE BUT COULD NOT. HE SWUNG IN MIDAIR FOR OVER AN HOUR, GETTING COLDER AND COLDER. HE LOOKED DOWN.

100 FEET (30.5 M) BELOW HIM WAS A HUGE CREVASSE.

YATES WAS DESPERATE. HE COULD NOT HOLD THE ROPE ANY LONGER. HE DIDN'T KNOW WHAT HAD HAPPENED TO JOE. HIS SNOW SEAT WAS CRUMBLING. HE WAS BEING PULLED OFF THE MOUNTAIN. YATES HAD ONLY ONE OPTION.

THE KNIFE! THERE'S A KNIFE IN MY BAG. IT'S THE ONLY WAY OUT! I'VE GOT TO CUT THE ROPE!

AHHHH!

SIMPSON DID NOT KNOW WHAT YATES HAD DONE, ONLY THAT HE WAS FALLING INTO A CREVASSE.

SIMPSON CRASHED THROUGH A SNOW BRIDGE, WHICH BROKE HIS FALL. HE SLID DOWN AN ICY SLOPE, COMING TO A STOP ON A LEDGE.

HE THOUGHT THAT YATES MUST HAVE FALLEN OFF THE MOUNTAIN AND WAS ON THE OTHER END OF THE ROPE, DEAD. HE PULLED ON IT UNTIL THE FREE END FELL INTO THE CREVASSE.

HE SAW THAT IT HAD BEEN CUT.

THIS MEANS THAT SIMON IS STILL ALIVE!

SIMPSON KNEW HE COULD NOT CLIMB OUT OF THE CREVASSE. HE COULD NOT STAY THERE, EITHER. HE HAD TO DESCEND FARTHER INTO THE CREVASSE AND HOPE THERE WAS ANOTHER ENTRANCE. HE CLIMBED INTO THE DARK HOLE.

SIMPSON REALIZED THAT IF HIS ROPE WAS NOT LONG ENOUGH, HE WOULD NOT BE ABLE TO CLIMB BACK UP.

THE ROPE WAS LONG ENOUGH. EVENTUALLY, SIMPSON WAS ON A SOLID SNOW FLOOR. IT WAS HIS FIFTH DAY ON THE MOUNTAIN.

MEANWHILE, SIMON YATES WAS TRYING TO GET BACK TO BASE CAMP. IT WAS A DIFFICULT AND DANGEROUS JOURNEY FOR ONE MAN. HE HAD SEEN THE CLIFF THAT HE HAD LOWERED SIMPSON OVER AND THE CREVASSE. HE FELT CERTAIN THAT HIS FRIEND WAS DEAD.

IN THE CREVASSE, WHAT SIMPSON THOUGHT WAS A SOLID FLOOR WAS NOT.

THAT SOUND - IT'S FALLING BLOCKS OF SNOW. THIS ISN'T THE FLOOR, IT'S THE CEILING! I HAVE TO GET TO SAFER GROUND.

SIMPSON LOOKED UP. HIGH ABOVE HIM HE SAW DAYLIGHT.

AN EXIT!

HE BEGAN THE PAINFUL CLIMB TOWARD THE OPENING.

AFTER MANY HOURS, SIMPSON BURST THROUGH SNOW AND INTO SUNSHINE.

BELOW HIM SIMPSON SAW FOOTPRINTS IN THE SNOW. THEY HAD BEEN MADE BY YATES ON HIS TREK BACK TO CAMP. SIMPSON FOLLOWED THEM TO THE MOUNTAIN'S GLACIER...

...AND THROUGH THE DEADLY CREVASSE FIELDS. HE WAS STILL SEVEN MILES (11.2 KM) FROM CAMP.

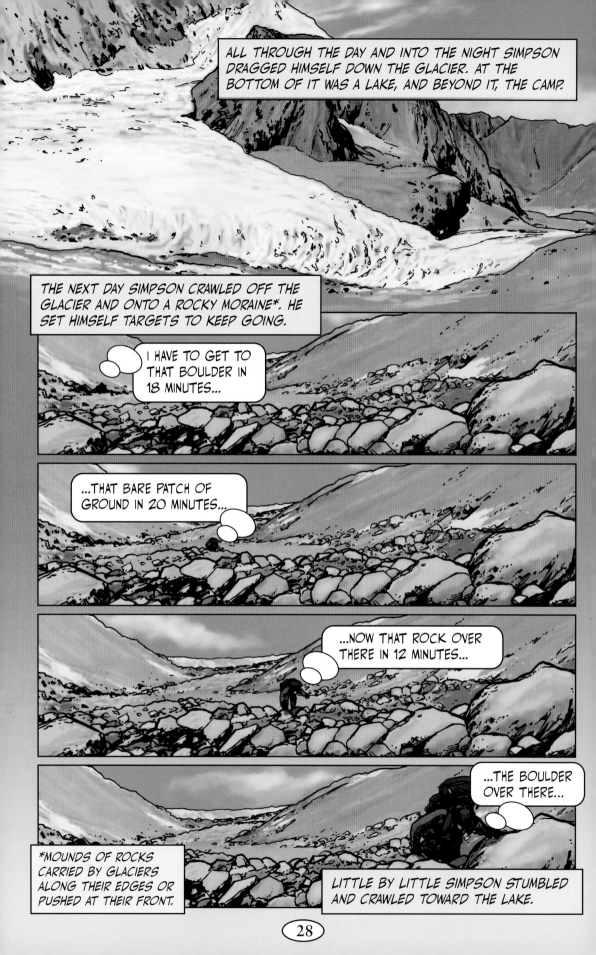

ALL THROUGH THE DAY AND INTO THE NIGHT SIMPSON DRAGGED HIMSELF DOWN THE GLACIER. AT THE BOTTOM OF IT WAS A LAKE, AND BEYOND IT, THE CAMP.

THE NEXT DAY SIMPSON CRAWLED OFF THE GLACIER AND ONTO A ROCKY MORAINE*. HE SET HIMSELF TARGETS TO KEEP GOING.

I HAVE TO GET TO THAT BOULDER IN 18 MINUTES...

...THAT BARE PATCH OF GROUND IN 20 MINUTES...

...NOW THAT ROCK OVER THERE IN 12 MINUTES...

...THE BOULDER OVER THERE...

*MOUNDS OF ROCKS CARRIED BY GLACIERS ALONG THEIR EDGES OR PUSHED AT THEIR FRONT.

LITTLE BY LITTLE SIMPSON STUMBLED AND CRAWLED TOWARD THE LAKE.

28

BACK AT THE CAMP SIMON YATES WAS RECOVERING FROM THE DESCENT. RICHARD HAWKING, WHO HAD BEEN GUARDING THEIR GEAR, WAS WITH HIM.

SIMON, YOU CAN'T BLAME YOURSELF FOR WHAT HAPPENED TO JOE. WE SHOULD BE THINKING ABOUT LEAVING.

YOU'RE RIGHT. WE'LL GO THE DAY AFTER TOMORROW.

SIMPSON WAS STILL ON THE MORAINE, AND HE WAS BECOMING VERY THIRSTY.

I CAN HEAR RUNNING WATER.

MELTWATER FROM THE GLACIER WAS TRICKLING BENEATH THE ROCKS. SIMPSON COULD HEAR IT, BUT IT WAS TOO DEEP FOR HIM TO REACH.

IT'S HERE SOMEWHERE!

SIMPSON SPENT THE NIGHT AMONG THE ROCKS. HE DID NOT THINK HE WOULD SURVIVE, BUT HE HAD TO KEEP TRYING.

THE NEXT MORNING SIMPSON FOUND WATER.

A FEW HOURS LATER HE REACHED THE LAKE. HE WOULD BE ABLE TO SEE THE CAMP FROM THE TOP OF THE MORAINE DAM.

I CAN DO THIS. I'M GOING TO BE ALL RIGHT.

BY LATE AFTERNOON HE HAD REACHED THE TOP OF THE DAM. IT WAS GETTING DARK, AND SNOW HAD BEGUN TO FALL.

I CAN'T SEE THE CAMP. MAYBE THEY'RE NOT THERE. MAYBE THEY'VE GONE!

SIMPSON CRAWLED AS FAR AS HE COULD. HE WAS EXHAUSTED AND COULD GO NO FURTHER, BUT HE KNEW THE CAMP WAS NEAR.

SIMON! SIMON!

YATES WOKE IN HIS TENT.

IS THAT JOE? IT CAN'T BE!

YATES AND HAWKINS RUSHED OUT INTO THE NIGHT.

THE SOUND CAME FROM OVER THERE!

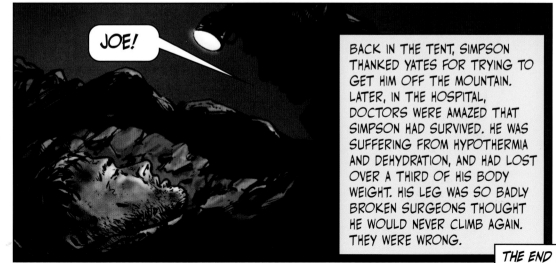

JOE!

BACK IN THE TENT, SIMPSON THANKED YATES FOR TRYING TO GET HIM OFF THE MOUNTAIN. LATER, IN THE HOSPITAL, DOCTORS WERE AMAZED THAT SIMPSON HAD SURVIVED. HE WAS SUFFERING FROM HYPOTHERMIA AND DEHYDRATION, AND HAD LOST OVER A THIRD OF HIS BODY WEIGHT. HIS LEG WAS SO BADLY BROKEN SURGEONS THOUGHT HE WOULD NEVER CLIMB AGAIN. THEY WERE WRONG.

THE END

# A LIFE-OR-DEATH DECISION
## ARON RALSTON, BLUE JOHN CANYON, UTAH, 2003

ON THE MORNING OF SATURDAY, APRIL 26, ARON RALSTON ENTERED BLUE JOHN CANYON. HE WAS ON A TREKKING AND CLIMBING VACATION IN UTAH'S CANYONLANDS NATIONAL PARK.

HE HAD NOT THOUGHT OF TELLING ANYONE WHERE HE WAS OR WHAT HE WAS DOING. HE WAS MORE USED TO SCALING THE MOUNTAINS OF COLORADO THAN SQUEEZING HIS WAY THROUGH THESE SLOT CANYONS*.

*SLOT CANYONS ARE MUCH DEEPER THAN THEY ARE WIDE. SOME CAN BE OVER 100 FEET (30 M) DEEP BUT LESS THAN 3 FEET (0.9 M) WIDE.

HE HAD NOT GONE FAR WHEN HE CAME TO A 9-FOOT (2.7-M) DROP. A SHORT DISTANCE FROM THE EDGE A ROCK WAS WEDGED BETWEEN THE CANYON WALLS.

ALL RALSTON HAD TO DO WAS GET ONTO THE BOULDER AND DROP TO THE CANYON FLOOR. HE CLIMBED OUT TO THE ROCK, STEPPED ONTO IT, AND CROUCHED DOWN.

THEN HE STARTED TO LOWER HIMSELF.

UH-OH!

SUDDENLY HE FELT THE ROCK MOVE. HIS WEIGHT HAD TWISTED IT LOOSE.

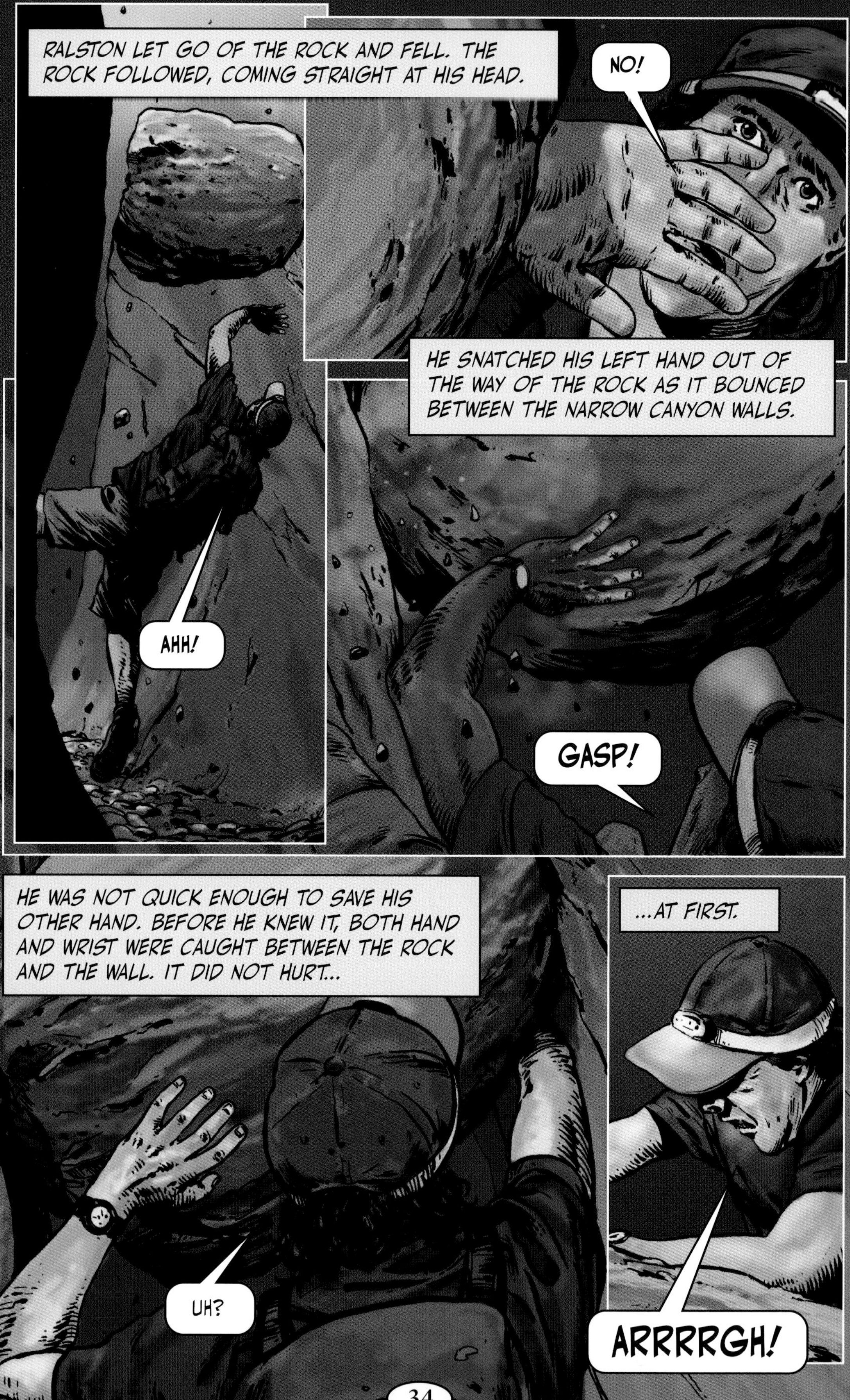
RALSTON LET GO OF THE ROCK AND FELL. THE ROCK FOLLOWED, COMING STRAIGHT AT HIS HEAD.
AHH!
NO!
HE SNATCHED HIS LEFT HAND OUT OF THE WAY OF THE ROCK AS IT BOUNCED BETWEEN THE NARROW CANYON WALLS.
GASP!
HE WAS NOT QUICK ENOUGH TO SAVE HIS OTHER HAND. BEFORE HE KNEW IT, BOTH HAND AND WRIST WERE CAUGHT BETWEEN THE ROCK AND THE WALL. IT DID NOT HURT...
UH?
...AT FIRST.
ARRRRGH!

RALSTON TRIED SHIFTING THE BOULDER OFF HIS HAND. HE COULDN'T MOVE IT.

NYEEAAARRG!

COME ON! MOVE!

HE EXAMINED THE DAMAGE THE BOULDER HAD DONE. HE COULD SEE HIS THUMB - IT WAS WHITE. THE ROCK HAD CUT OFF ITS BLOOD SUPPLY. THE HAND HAD BECOME NUMB AND HAD STOPPED HURTING.

THE BOULDER MUST WEIGH OVER 800 POUNDS*. MY HAND IS HOLDING IT AWAY FROM THE WALL.

*363 KILOGRAMS

RALSTON EMPTIED HIS BACKPACK TO SEE WHAT SUPPLIES HE HAD.

CD PLAYER, CDS, CAMCORDER, CAMERA, SPARE BATTERIES, SUNGLASSES, HEADLAMP, CLIMBING GEAR, BURRITOS, AND ABOUT A PINT OF WATER.

I CAN GET BY WITHOUT FOOD - BUT WATER? THIS WON'T LAST MORE THAN A COUPLE OF DAYS. THEN I'VE GOT TWO OR THREE DAYS, MAXIMUM.

HE ALSO HAD A MULTITOOL - A PAIR OF PLIERS, TWO BLADES, AND A FILE ALL IN ONE.

NO ONE'S GOING TO FIND ME HERE BY ACCIDENT. I'M GOING TO HAVE TO GET MYSELF OUT. IF I CAN CUT ENOUGH ROCK AWAY I CAN FREE MY HAND.

HE BEGAN CHIPPING AT THE ROCK WITH THE MULTITOOL BLADE. HE KEPT AT IT UNTIL LATE SATURDAY NIGHT, AND HE WAS GETTING TIRED.

35

IT TOOK OVER TWO DOZEN TRIES BEFORE THE KNOT LANDED IN THE CRACK ABOVE RALSTON'S HEAD. HE GAVE THE ROPE A FIRM TUG, WEDGING IT INTO THE GAP.

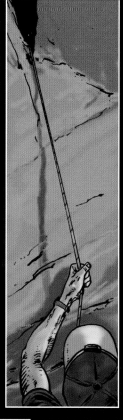

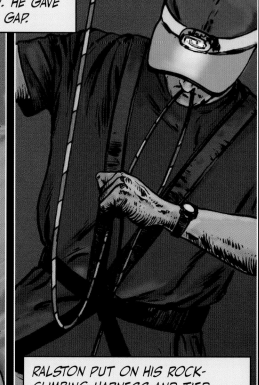

RALSTON PUT ON HIS ROCK-CLIMBING HARNESS AND TIED THE FREE END OF THE ROPE TO IT. HE HAD MADE HIMSELF A SEAT.

FOR THE FIRST TIME IN TWELVE HOURS RALSTON COULD TAKE SOME OF THE WEIGHT OFF HIS LEGS.

AHHHH!

HE CHIPPED AWAY AT THE ROCK THROUGHOUT THE NIGHT.

ON SUNDAY MORNING RALSTON JUDGED HIS PROGRESS. IT WAS NOT GOOD.

THE ROCK'S TOO TOUGH. AT THIS RATE IT'S GOING TO TAKE SIX DAYS TO GET MY HAND FREE. I DON'T HAVE THAT MUCH TIME. I NEED A NEW PLAN.

RALSTON HOOKED A ROPE OVER A JUTTING ROCK ABOVE HIS HEAD. HE LOOPED THE OTHER END AROUND THE BOULDER.

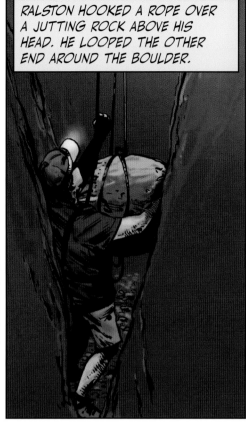

HE HAD MANAGED TO RIG UP A PULLEY SYSTEM. RALSTON HAULED ON THE ROPE...

GRUNT!

...BUT THE ROCK DID NOT BUDGE. ON MONDAY HE GAVE UP TRYING. LATER, RALSTON DRANK THE LAST FEW DROPS OF HIS WATER AND FOR THE FIRST TIME THOUGHT ABOUT CUTTING OFF HIS OWN ARM.

HACKING AT THE ROCK HAS BLUNTED THE BIG BLADE.

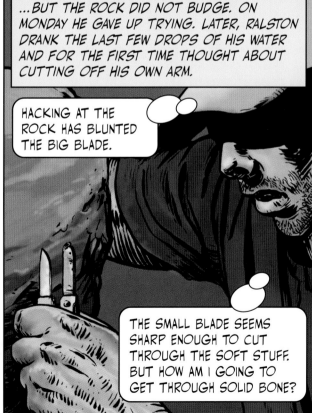

THE SMALL BLADE SEEMS SHARP ENOUGH TO CUT THROUGH THE SOFT STUFF. BUT HOW AM I GOING TO GET THROUGH SOLID BONE?

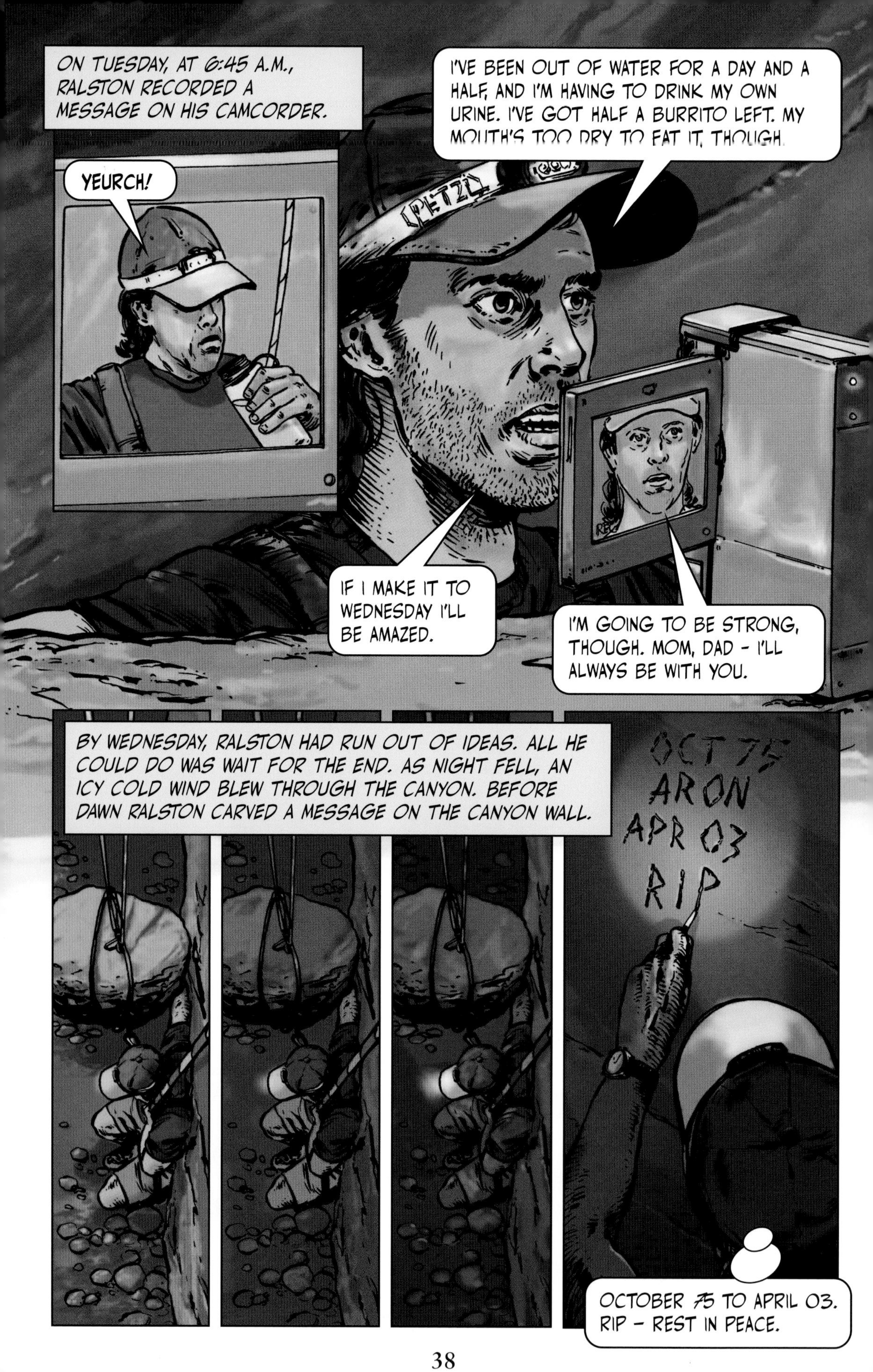
ON TUESDAY, AT 6:45 A.M., RALSTON RECORDED A MESSAGE ON HIS CAMCORDER.
YEURCH!
I'VE BEEN OUT OF WATER FOR A DAY AND A HALF, AND I'M HAVING TO DRINK MY OWN URINE. I'VE GOT HALF A BURRITO LEFT. MY MOUTH'S TOO DRY TO EAT IT, THOUGH.
IF I MAKE IT TO WEDNESDAY I'LL BE AMAZED.
I'M GOING TO BE STRONG, THOUGH. MOM, DAD - I'LL ALWAYS BE WITH YOU.
BY WEDNESDAY, RALSTON HAD RUN OUT OF IDEAS. ALL HE COULD DO WAS WAIT FOR THE END. AS NIGHT FELL, AN ICY COLD WIND BLEW THROUGH THE CANYON. BEFORE DAWN RALSTON CARVED A MESSAGE ON THE CANYON WALL.
OCT 75
ARON
APR 03
RIP
OCTOBER 75 TO APRIL 03. RIP - REST IN PEACE.

ON THURSDAY MORNING, RALSTON USED HIS KNIFE TO BRUSH GRIT FROM CUTS ON HIS TRAPPED HAND. THE BLADE ACCIDENTALLY PUNCTURED HIS THUMB.

GASSES ESCAPED FROM THE HAND. IT HAD STARTED TO ROT. HE REALIZED THAT EVEN IF HE WERE RESCUED HE WOULD LOSE HIS HAND. IN FRUSTRATION AND RAGE, RALSTON YANKED AT HIS ARM, TRYING TO WRENCH IT FREE.

*SSSSSHHHHH!*

UGH! THE SMELL!

I JUST WANT TO GET RID OF IT!

AS HE THREW HIMSELF ACROSS THE ROCK, A PAIN SHOT THROUGH HIS TRAPPED WRIST.

OWW!

AN IDEA CAME TO HIM.

THAT'S IT! THAT'S HOW I'M GOING TO GET OUT OF HERE!

IF THE BONES IN HIS ARM WERE BROKEN, HE WOULD NOT NEED TO CUT THROUGH THEM. RALSTON PUT HIS LEFT HAND UNDER THE ROCK TO ACT AS A LEVER.

COME ON! LET'S DO IT!

"...ACKK! ACKK!"

KERRACKK!!

KERR...ACKK!!

ONE!...

TWO!...

THREE! AARRRGHHH!

RALSTON PUSHED DOWN HARD TO HIS LEFT. WITH A SNAP, THE LARGE BONE IN HIS FOREARM SHATTERED. HE PUSHED AGAIN, AND THE SMALLER BONE BROKE. IT WAS 10:32 A.M. HE DID NOT STOP. HE GRABBED HIS MULTITOOL...

...AND GOT TO WORK.

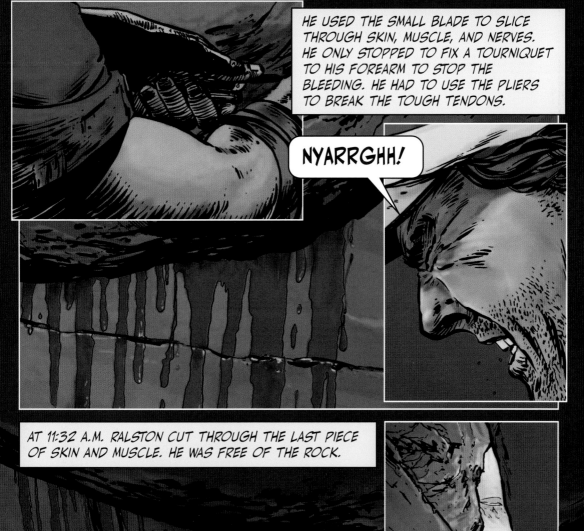

HE USED THE SMALL BLADE TO SLICE THROUGH SKIN, MUSCLE, AND NERVES. HE ONLY STOPPED TO FIX A TOURNIQUET TO HIS FOREARM TO STOP THE BLEEDING. HE HAD TO USE THE PLIERS TO BREAK THE TOUGH TENDONS.

NYARRGHH!

AT 11:32 A.M. RALSTON CUT THROUGH THE LAST PIECE OF SKIN AND MUSCLE. HE WAS FREE OF THE ROCK.

OOF!

RALSTON COULD NOT WASTE TIME. HE MADE A SLING FOR HIS ARM AND SET OFF UP THE CANYON.

TWENTY MINUTES LATER RALSTON WAS STANDING ON THE LIP OF THE BIG DROP RAPPEL, A 70-FOOT-TALL (21.3-M) CLIFF FACE. HE WAS OUT OF THE SLOT CANYON.

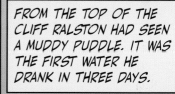

FROM THE TOP OF THE CLIFF RALSTON HAD SEEN A MUDDY PUDDLE. IT WAS THE FIRST WATER HE DRANK IN THREE DAYS.

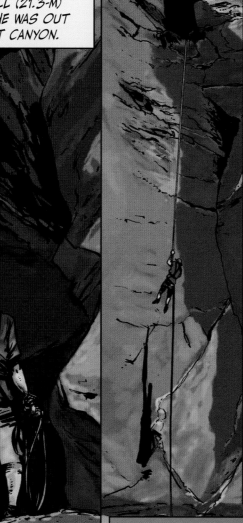

RALSTON KNEW HE WAS NOT SAFE. HIS TRUCK WAS EIGHT MILES (12.8 KM) AWAY, AND IN SPITE OF THE TOURNIQUET HIS ARM WAS BLEEDING. HE NEEDED TO FIND HELP.

AFTER WALKING FOR SIX MILES (9.6 KM), RALSTON SAW THREE HIKERS, THE MEIJER FAMILY.

HELP!

MY NAME IS ARON RALSTON. A BOULDER TRAPPED MY ARM ON SATURDAY AND I HAVEN'T EATEN OR HAD ANYTHING TO DRINK FOR FIVE DAYS.

I CUT MY ARM OFF THIS MORNING TO GET FREE, AND I'VE LOST A LOT OF BLOOD. I NEED TO GET TO A HOSPITAL.

THE AUTHORITIES HAD BEEN SEARCHING FOR RALSTON IN THE CANYONLANDS NATIONAL PARK ALL MORNING. THEY HAD TRACED HIM THERE THROUGH HIS CREDIT CARD PURCHASES AND HAD ALSO FOUND HIS TRUCK. AT 3:00 P.M. A HELICOPTER FINALLY RESCUED HIM. HE SPENT MANY WEEKS IN THE HOSPITAL RECOVERING FROM HIS ORDEAL.

1:30 P.M. MARCH 9, 2005. MOUNT EOLUS, COLORADO.

TWO YEARS AFTER HIS ORDEAL, ARON RALSTON REACHED THE SUMMIT OF MOUNT EOLUS. HE BECAME THE FIRST PERSON TO CLIMB ALL OF COLORADO'S 59 FOURTEENERS* ALONE AND IN THE WINTER.

*FOURTEENERS ARE MOUNTAINS THAT ARE 14,000 FEET (4,267 M) OR HIGHER.

THE END

# MORE SURVIVAL STORIES

Here are three more true stories of survival in mountain regions.

### K2, THE SAVAGE MOUNTAIN

The Third American Karakoram Expedition arrived at their base camp on June 20, 1953. The expedition, led by Charles Houston, was in the Himalayas to climb K2. At 28,251 feet (8,611 m) K2 was then the world's tallest unclimbed mountain. It had a reputation for being dangerous to climb and had claimed many lives. In spite of the hazards, the eight-man team began the ascent and by August 1, had set up a camp at 25,500 feet (7,800 m).

They were about to start the final push for the summit when a storm broke. For days the eight climbers were trapped on the mountain. After a week, even though the weather had begun to improve, they still could not go on.

One of the climbers, Art Gilkey, had become dangerously ill. They decided to bring him down the mountain. The storm was getting worse again, and there was a risk of avalanches. They placed Gilkey in a sleeping bag and started the descent.

They had not gone far when one of the climbers fell, pulling his rope-mate with him. They in turn pulled others with them. Soon six climbers were falling down the mountainside. At the end of the rope was Pete Schoening. He wrapped the line around his shoulders and ice ax before he too fell, and halted the mass fall. All the climbers returned safely to base camp except for Gilkey, who was swept away in an avalanche. His body was found in 1993.

## A Stay at the Middle Peak Hotel

At 12,316 feet (3,754 m) Aoroki/Mount Cook on New Zealand's South Island is the country's highest mountain and a popular destination for climbers. In 1982 New Zealanders Mark Inglis and Phil Doole were close to its summit when a blizzard hit them. All they could do was dig a snow cave and wait in it for the storm to end.

They called the hole the Middle Peak Hotel and spent 13 nights there. In that time they ran out of food, and their legs became badly frostbitten. When they were eventually rescued, both men lost their legs below the knees. However, Mark Inglis did not view this as a hindrance. In 2000 he won a silver medal at a cycling event at the Sydney Paralympics and in 2006 became the first person with prosthetic legs to climb Mount Everest.

## Swept Away

It was June 1997. Colby Coombs and two friends, Tom Walter and Ritt Kellogg were climbing Mount Foraker in Alaska when an avalanche hit them, knocking them 1,000 feet (304 m) down the mountain. When Coombs awoke he was still attached to his rope. He had broken his ankle, shoulder blade, and neck. Hanging limply a few feet away was the body of Tom Walter, and the following day he would find the body of Ritt Kellog. Coombs began a painful crawl back to base camp. It took him four days.

# GLOSSARY

**avalanche** A fall or slide of a large amount of snow or rock down a mountainside.

**blizzard** A violent snowstorm with strong winds.

**canyon** A narrow, deep opening with steep cliff walls, cut into the earth by running water.

**crampons** A spiked metal framework that is attached to the bottom of a shoe or boot to prevent slipping when climbing on ice or snow.

**crevasse** A deep crack or opening in a glacier.

**dam** A barrier that prevents the flow of water.

**dehydration** Loss of bodily fluids from lack of water.

**destination** The place set for the end of a journey.

**erosion** The process of wearing or grinding something down by the movement of particles.

**frostbite** The freezing of a part of the body which causes damage.

**fuselage** The central body of an aircraft, to which the wings and tail are attached.

**glacier** A huge mass of ice that flows slowly down a mountain or valley.

**hazard** A source of danger.

**hindrance** Something that prevents something happening or someone from doing something.

**hypothermia** The condition caused by a person's body temperature falling below 95°F (35°C). This can happen at temperatures above freezing as well as below freezing.

**isolation** Being far away from other places or people.

**jutting** To extend out beyond a surface.

**ordeal** A severe experience.

**perilous** Full of danger.

**pliers** A small instrument with two handles and two jaws, used for holding, bending or cutting something.

**prosthetic** An artificial part used to replace a part of the body that has been removed.

**pulley** A simple machine consisting of a wheel with a grooved rim through which a rope can be pulled.

**summit** The top of a mountain.

**tourniquet** A tight bandage that stops the flow of blood by applying pressure.

# FOR MORE INFORMATION

## ORGANIZATIONS

**American Alpine Institute**
1515 12th Street
Bellingham
WA 98225
(360) 671 1505
Web site: http://www.aai.cc

**The Geological Society of America**
PO Box 9104
Boulder
CO 80301-9140
(303) 357 1000
Web site: http://www.geosociety.org

## FURTHER READING

Chester, Jonathan. *Young Adventurers' Guide to Everest: From Avalanche to Zopkio*. Berkeley, CA: Tricycle Press, 2005.

Crompton, Samuel Willard. *Sir Edmund Hillary* (Great Explorers). New York, NY: Chelsea House Publications, 2009.

Gill, Shelley. *Adventure at the Bottom of the World, Adventure at the Top of the World*. Seattle, WA: Sasquatch Books/Paws IV Children's Books, 2002.

Masoff, Joy. *Everest: Reaching for the Sky*. New York, NY: Scholastic Paperbacks, 2002.

Oxlade, Chris. *Rock Climbing* (Extreme Sports). Minneapolis, MN: Lerner Publishing Group, 2003.

Stephens, Rebecca. *Everest* (DK Eyewitness Books). London, England: DK Children, 2001.

# INDEX

## Web Sites

Due to the changing nature of Internet links, Rosen Publishing has developed an online list of Web sites related to the subject of this book. This site is updated regularly. Please use this link to access the list:

http://www.rosenlinks.com/ddss/moun